Guess What

Published in the United States of America by
Cherry Lake Publishing
Ann Arbor, Michigan
www.cherrylakepublishing.com

Content Adviser: Susan Heinrichs Gray
Reading Adviser: Marla Conn, ReadAbility, Inc.
Book Design: Felicia Macheske

Photo Credits: © Eric Isselée/Shutterstock.com, cover, 3, 4, 9, 11, 15, 17, 21, back cover; © davemhuntphotography/
Shutterstock.com, 1; © kao/Shutterstock.com, 6; © Claudia Otte/Shutterstock.com, 12; © e2dan/Shutterstock.com, 18;
© Andrey_Kuzmin/Shutterstock.com, back cover

Library of Congress Cataloging-in-Publication Data

Calhoun, Kelly, author.
 Fiercely feline / Kelly Calhoun.
 pages cm. — (Guess what)
 Summary: "Young children are natural problem solvers and always looking for answers, especially when it involves animals.
Guess What: Fiercely Feline: Lion provides young curious readers with striking visual clues and simply written hints. Using the
photos and text, readers rely on visual literacy skills, reading, and reasoning as they solve the animal mystery. Clearly written
facts give readers a deeper understanding of how the animal lives. Additional text features, including a glossary and an index,
help students locate information and learn new words."— Provided by publisher.
 Audience: Age 5
 Audience: K to grade 3
 Includes index.
 ISBN 978-1-63362-623-2 (hardcover) — ISBN 978-1-63362-713-0 (pbk.) — ISBN 978-1-63362-803-8 (pdf) —
ISBN 978-1-63362-893-9 (ebook)
 1. Lion—Juvenile literature. 2. Children's questions and answers. I. Title.

 QL737.C23C342 2016
 599.757—dc23

 2015003093

33614059685106

Cherry Lake Publishing would like to acknowledge the work of The Partnership for 21st Century Skills.
Please visit *www.p21.org* for more information.

Printed in the United States of America
Corporate Graphics Inc.

Table of Contents

I have eyes that can see in the dark.

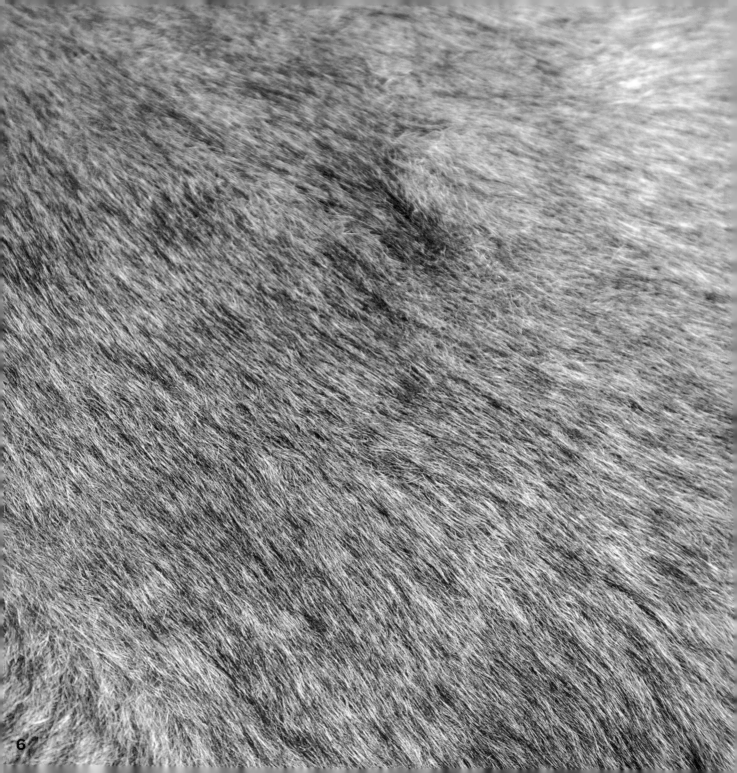

My body is covered with fur.

I have a thick mane.

I rest almost **20 hours** a day.

ZZZZZZZZZ

I have big paws with sharp claws.

I have a tuft on the end of my tail.

I have long, sharp fangs.

CHOMP!

I have
a loud
ROAR!

Do you know what I am?

About Lions

1. A lion's roar can be heard up to 5 miles away.

2. Male lions have manes. Female lions do not.

3. Lions live in large groups called prides.

4. A lion might **hunt** for 3 or 4 hours a day.

5. Lions can see in the dark.

Glossary

fangs (fangz) an animal's long, pointed teeth

hunt (huhnt) to chase and kill other animals for food

mane (mayn) the long, thick hair on the head and neck of lions and some other animals

roar (ror) to make a loud, deep, prolonged sound

tuft (tuhft) a bunch of individual pieces of something such as hair that are attached together at the bottom

Index